Jennifer and Claerwen Holland

Jennifer and Claerwen Holland have lived all their lives in the same house on the Welsh borders, in Powys. Claerwen is an artist who has regular exhibitions; Jennifer is a gifted poet with an eye for the everyday details of home and garden.

Jennifer Holland

A YEAR AND A DAY

With drawings by
Claerwen Holland

Of all the creatures both in sea and land
Only to man thou hast made known thy wayes
And put the penne alone into his hand
And made him secretarie of thy praise . . .
George Herbert

Jennifer Holland
Claerwen Holland.

Cover photograph of the Authors by A. J. Willfad

First published in Great Britain 1990

Spire is an imprint of Hodder & Stoughton *Publishers*

British Library Cataloguing in Publication Data

Holland, Jennifer
A year and a day.
I. Title
821.914

ISBN 0-340-53853-8

Printed in Great Britain for Hodder and Stoughton Limited, Mill Road, Dunton Green, Sevenoaks, Kent by Clays Limited, St Ives plc. Photoset by Rowland Phototypesetting Limited, Bury St Edmunds, Suffolk.

Hodder and Stoughton Editorial Office: 47 Bedford Square, London WC1B 3DP.

To Michael Green, who inspired this book.

Contents

Autumn

Foreword
by Canon Michael Green

Come with me in imagination to a fine grey stone house up a curving drive in the heart of mid-Wales. If you are not Welsh you will probably not be able even to pronounce, let alone spell the name of the tiny village of Cwmdauddwr where the house is situated, commanding superb views of the rolling hills and green fields, with hardly a dwelling in sight. You knock on the door and it opens to usher you into the presence of three people: Elisabeth Holland, who owns the estate which has been in her family for many generations, with her daughters Claerwen, a sensitive and widely acclaimed artist, and Jennifer who writes evocative poetry. I have had the privilege of knowing this family for many years, and they have become dear and generous friends. Many is the day I have been utterly renewed by fishing a stretch of the Wye whose rights they own, and which they have so kindly afforded me. So I have got to know and love them well, and am delighted to have the opportunity to commend this most unusual book. How often have you come across a book both of poetry and painting written by two such sisters? I know of no other case. And it will bring the peace and contentment of that background in rural Wales to many hearts that are pressurised by the pace of modern life. This is a gracious book, one to which I think you are likely often to return. I know I shall!

Michael Green
Regent College
Vancouver

Introduction

This book is intended to share some of the delight Claerwen and I, as writer and painter, have found in the Welsh border country and a year's rhythm of life there, and to be a record of some of the things and places which during the last decade have become increasingly threatened.

We live in the centre of a farming, and an essentially sheep-farming, community. Sheep, sheepdogs and hens have been part of our lives from earliest childhood. I remember particularly a tame hen which used to accompany us on walks when we were very small, preceded by one of the dynasty of backdoor cats, also so much a feature of our childhood.

I have been writing poetry ever since I was nine years old, and Claerwen has been painting since early childhood. The drawings which accompany the poems in this book, done with ink and a matchstick, are not always intended as a literal depiction of them. As the painter Matisse wrote, 'A painter and writer should work together without confusion, on parallel lines. The drawings should be the plastic equivalent of a poem.'

One of my favourite poems is 'Farewell' by Walter de la Mare, especially the lines 'Look thy last on all things lovely every hour . . .' Because the Welsh border country is still so little spoilt there is a fear of its losing its specialness: a struggle between the need to make a living from the land and the imperative claims of conservation.

Other poets from this part of Wales have also felt its potent magic, and we have chosen quotes from three of them who were aware of the spiritual dimension of this countryside with its everchanging light on the hills, to link our Year and a Day. Henry Vaughan, known as the Silurist, lived by Llangorse

Lake in Breconshire; Thomas Traherne, the mystic, lived over the border in Herefordshire; and George Herbert, the parson poet, was brought up in Monmouthshire.

Even in the seventeenth century there were intimations of man's irrepressible thrust for change in the name of progress: 'It [the world] is a region of light and peace, did not men disquiet it', Thomas Traherne wrote.

Opening up the countryside with ever wider roads and bigger cars is a part of sharing, and yet I feel so much that the privacy of what speaks of another world should be fostered and maintained and that artists of whatever discipline – painting, music, sculpture, poetry – should bear a part in keeping stable a way of life and its sense of faith that has endured for centuries.

Philip Larkin declared that he made it a rule never to write about other forms of art. On the contrary, I have frequently felt the need to write about those whose visions have touched a sympathy of mine: Robin Tanner, Reynolds Stone, Laurence Whistler . . . Art and poetry have such an empathy with each other, a meeting of the spirit, that their fused message is often the same.

'Walk with thy fellow-creatures: note the hush/And whispers amongst them . . .' In this landscape where the Border Poets were so much concerned with noting the 'hush and whispers' among their fellow creatures – the birds, the insects and the forgotten things in the hedgerows – it would be good if this book too could have borne a part in keeping these things in remembrance.

Jennifer Holland

Prologue

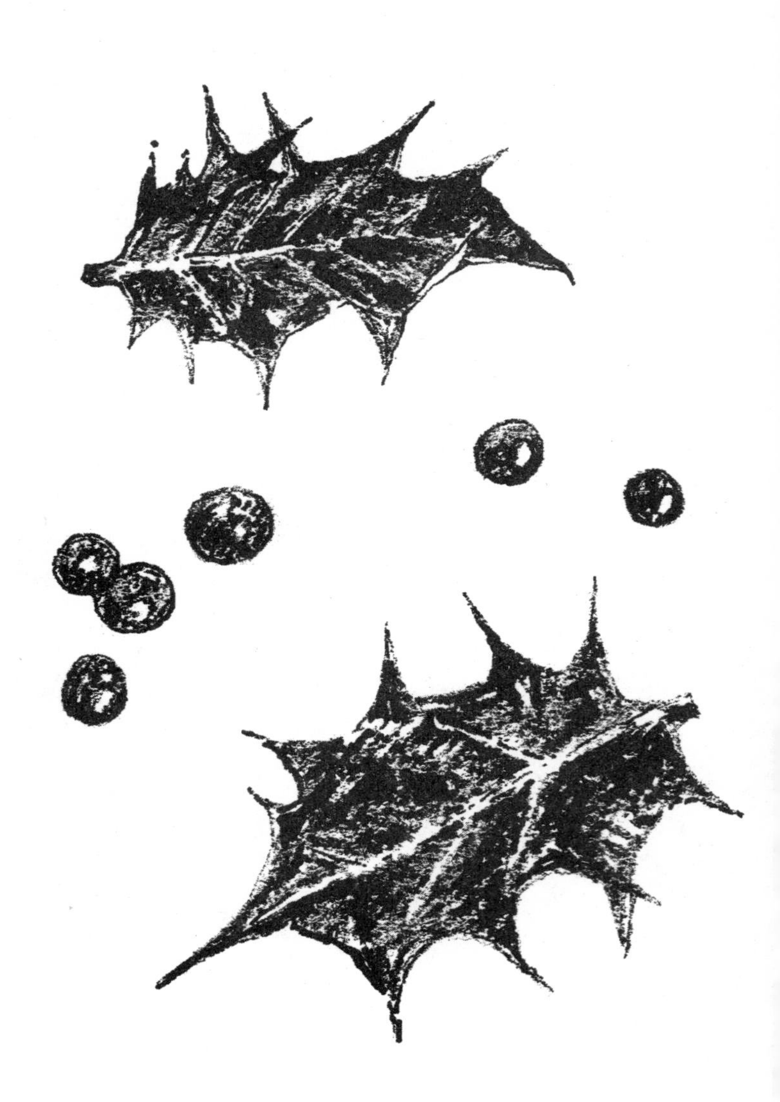

THOUGHTS ON NEW YEAR

In this black beginning time
We're aware of the inexorable triangle:
Past, present and future –
Inexorable as the holy triangle
Of Father, Mother and Child.
The Father, the god-figure, rises
Solid from the past,
Like the up-pushing hills or the core-straight oaks.
The Mother, nursing her first-born,
Is content to guard over the present,
Uniting all the hopes and terrors,
All the staggering pain of creation,
Into the immediacy of the feeding Child.
The Child turns from his Mother
With a face noon-sun bright,
Blessing the future where all time must go –
The time that dances to heaven's equal music
In the black beginning of the year.

Spring

By the very right of your senses
You enjoy the world.
Thomas Traherne

Hark! How his winds have chang'd their note,
And with warm whispers call thee out.
The frosts are past, the storms are gone:
And backward life at last comes on.
Henry Vaughan

And round beneath it
Time in hours, days, years
Driv'n by the spheres
Like a vast shadow mov'd . . .
Henry Vaughan

Man is one world and hath
Another to attend him.
George Herbert

LIGHT

It was the first thing, fingering over chaos;
Streaking across the water in a white ribbon
Until gradually the whole earth was dancing, dancing
Under the widening line of it vibrating through
the water and sand.

And darkness squeezed in again as the spheres moved
Imperceptibly, year on year.
And the flame in the closeness was little, yet lambent,
And wavered but was not quenched.

For darkness cannot gainsay
The unstoppable pulse of light upon the waters,
Dictating the rhythm where life must go.

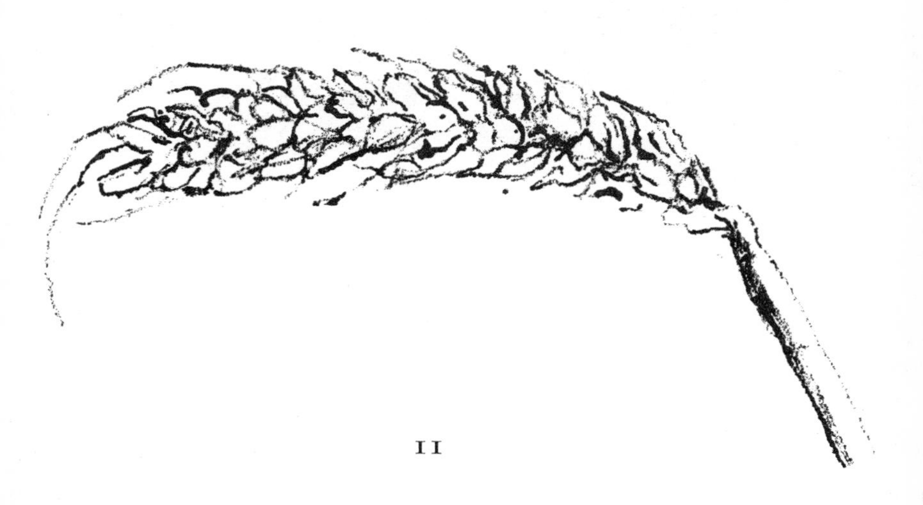

GARDENS

In the beginning was the garden and light,
The sun, like a giant apple,
Hanging over the tree,
Gilding the long coiled rope of the serpent's tail;
Touching the woman's hair into a rosy glory,
Illuming every sinew of the man's numbered
muscles . . .

Dusk in the garden,
Shadows touching the Man for pity;
Strained light moving over the knot of people
Who sleep under the olive trees
Feathered by night;
While the tender plants
Sweat in sorrowful dew.

Dawn in the garden
As the cock crew.
Dawn in the world
Where life stirs for ever . . .

SPRING

It stretches in the snort of a gale,
Like a great golden calf,
Among a glazed spread of buttercups . . .
Everywhere things sacrificial, youthfully
appealing,
Feeling the sun's first awakening of power;
Its mountain-shaking enthusiasm
All the shining potential of a
New winter-forgotten world . . .

Yet there's a wobblingness in the gambolling;
Occasional uncertainty,
As if new life apprehends the knife,
And white doom of summer:
A dream dread to colour the living,
The joy of these not-unheeding creatures . . .

Youth's claimed to be so immaturely wasted
Upon the totter-head young –
Is the clamouring, burgeoning, rook-ranged spring
Wasted upon a world
Of self-induced wastage?

KILVERT AT CLYRO

Girls with brook bright faces
And corn-glad hair
Tumbling over pinafores
That are fresh as falls of snow;
And the hills urging a tramp to Cabalva
Under a changeful sky
To the encouragement of a clamour of curlews;
A whistle of larks . . .

Valentine cards
Fretted over with lace
Like mailings of hoar-frosts;
Sermons rehearsed to tabby Toby;
Then a stamp of boots on stairs
To bring cheer with a Bible word;
A God-given smile . . .
Old tales to hear,
Rare as long exchanged coins;
Past-earthly griefs to soothe;
Croquet and archery tournaments to attend
And drawing-room closenesses to observe
On moon-told nights . . .

Look, a fall of stars:
Easter-risen primroses;
And a transposition of sky
In a pool of fair weather bluebells.

PEMBROKESHIRE WALK

Campion stars the wall banks
And bluebells curl
Their tender heads fernwards;
Over all gulls hurl
Their screaming flight across shoreline,
Rising, a lark sings
Spinning away, away
On vibrant wings;
And the paths are full
Of insects and hiding things.

The sea's a magic-touched green;
Through sea-fret islands float;
And the shore is busy with
Dogs, children, a boat.
Far distant a cuckoo calls
With unending note.
A jet races over the cliffs
Rasping above the gale;
And the sands, in brown, storm dust
Rustle a secret tale . . .

THE DAY AFTER

Spread up the table
With once-tasted ham,
Pink as a peony;
Chicken and grapes,
And marble-like new potatoes cram
All rounded that are left
Fairly upon two plates.

Remains of orange mousse,
Light as a cloud-cap;
Stained-glass fruit salad
Piled into each bowl:
Remnants of feasting
Given second life,
Fragments of one, savouringly eaten, whole.

Avocados, unforgotten in their spring dress
And cheese and biscuits
Creaming up on the plate;
Real coffee and one chance discovered mint found
To finish off this gourmet's pickings meal;
This dwindled company's treat:
A note from concerto's sound.

And with the second-chance food
We find our thinking
Dwelling upon what we last dinnertime said:
The fun we drew
From scraps of rag-bag tellings,
Golden wine talk
Poured from a bottle new.

CAVE IN HAFOD WOODS

Here, in flights of leaping crystal,
Nimue might have ravished Merlin,
For the waterfall cave was something apart from time,
Slippery with unspent magic,
Echoing with the water's skeined-up foam;
While outside the scrambling wood
Tumbled itself into a turret of sunshine.

In the cave with its necromancy of quick legends
The pure down-rush of the falls
Made oblation to the gilded gods
Who twist up the waters and trees
Into undying worship
In this tragedy-touched
Welsh wood.

IN TRUST

It's the small things I'd miss losing most:
Violets in a peace of blue stars;
Wrens, up and down like lace bobbins,
The finished lace of spiders' webs,
And the thread thrown by the gently-horned snail.

The bulldozers level the bluebells
In a clearing of *their* world,
And a new road dodges through a hamlet
Spinning an artery of death . . .
The camera-primed invade
Each secret oasis
And their trophied orchids
Wilt in the green air.

We've all read the books, the magazines, seen the telly –
The country is as inexorably ours
As a name-tag on a new baby.
Our child.
It exists for us –
From the Romans to the Second Elizabethans
We have mangled it, shredded it,
Picked at it, slaughtered it,
Sprayed it, photographed it,
Painted it, written sonnets to it . . .
Now we are its ultimate destiny:
Plundering, reckless, lovingly curious hands
Making clumsy thrusts to save it.

PIED FLYCATCHERS

They spun, dipped, caught their precious meals,
Flying like uncurled leaves or snow
Swift swirling, with a dash of soot;
With following eyes too slow

To catch their instant, feathery joy,
Yet, with binoculars raised,
We watched the young brood's tumbling start,
Mid-afternoon, rain-hazed . . .

A shy invasion, we were honoured,
This summer of the birds;
When daily thrush has sung his song
In operas without words.

BEING IS LIVING

Cabbages grow because you want them to;
Guiding the unfolding senses,
Sharing worlds of pirates and giants and princes
Can be as new-creating
As nine-to-five behind plate-glass;
The nun's bent knees
And caring God rest
As vital for the nation
As scurrying bells at Westminster . . .

'So useless!' but numb in a hospital bed
Is part of the joining of the
Wisdom of heaven;
And the unemployed,
Far from the jangle-jungle life
Of the next plane to Frankfurt,
Listen to the blackbird
In a small vivid adventure of the spirit.

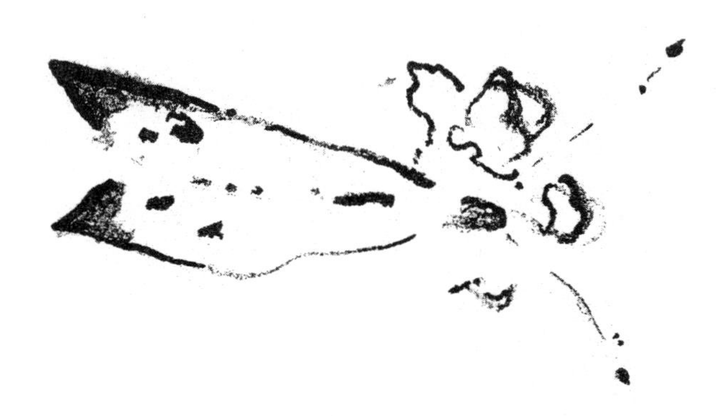

Summer

Fresh fields and woods! the Earth's fair face,
God's footstool, and man's dwelling-place.
Henry Vaughan

. . . For each day
The Valley, or the Mountain
Afforded visits, and still Paradise lay
In some green shade, or fountain.
Henry Vaughan

And in those weaker glories spy
Some shadow of eternity . . .
Henry Vaughan

Thou canst not misse his Praise; each
tree, herb, flowre
Are shadows of his wisdome, and his pow'r.
Henry Vaughan

You never enjoy the world aright till the sea
itself floweth in your veins, till you are clothed
with the heavens and crowned with the stars . . .
Thomas Traherne

THE MOTIONLESS TREE

'A Tree being motionless birds come to it.' A Bleddfa saying

In the beginning grew a tree,
Fruit came to it
And birds came to the fruit.

And a Man came to the tree
And hung there, motionless, and
Birds flew to Him . . .

To this Tree of Man
Flew birds like loosed arrows
For pity in creation:

Birds of joy of life, of creative force;
Birds reflecting back
Their supreme trust in their creator.

And the tree
Was motionless in their activity,
And blossomed
With the fruits of their spirits.

HOTEL BREAKFAST

Warily the guests creak down the carpeted stair
To take possession of the dining room;
Trying to feel in the mood for the eggs and bacon
They have in the evening at home . . .

Sparkle up, blue day,
Lay a possessive light
Over the Torygraphs
Overspread on each table;
Knock glints off the cheering juice,
And high fibre cereal,
The Oxford marmalade
And sand-coloured toast . . .

Now's the moment to:
Rev up the cameras,
The water colours,
The bird books –
The sun's roused up to strike . . .

'Good morning!' But they don't say it;
In possession of it they smile wary-dog smiles,
And forget obligations in their struggles with the
cornflakes . . .

Away over the estuary the male-dancer gulls
Chortle throatily;
The early boats slip out –
It's waiting for them;
And they hug the realisation of it to themselves
Over the gritty, speckled dregs of their coffee.

THE HIDDEN GARDEN

Sun skitters on a hazy maze of raspberry canes,
Drawing out gold from the Cotswold roof slates;
And the carrots wave their tops
Like green feathers in the dusk blowing wind.
Swallows flicker and fly catch, and swifts squeak, flying
pondwards;
And the gooseberries, under their nets, are small globed cat's
eyes of colour . . .

Angled roof and ripe kitchen garden –
Who would spend a fortune in the tropics
With such a secret view?
It would magic me homewards
In its Beatrix Potter green and gold,
Triumphing over bone-coloured beaches,
And wine-coloured, ever-polluted seas.

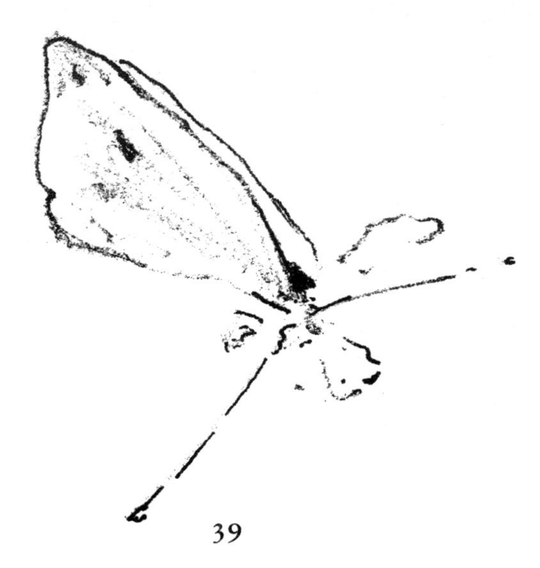

SHELLING PEAS

Summer rosaries
Clicking gently, Mary-like,
Through Martha's fingers.

SUMMER SUNDAY

A votive peace swings down
Among the tumble head naves of grasses
And sappy, stained-glass blue of bluebells.
Here the bumble bees drone and chant
Hotly, spicily,
And pigeons groan amens for ever.
The fan-vault bridal-fingered cowparsley
Shivers above me in a prodigal whiteness . . .

Far away the tinted glass,
The water-cold stone;
Spread out in this Cotswold wood
I could raise a lark storm of song to heaven;
An outpouring of warm, earth-praising thanksgiving.

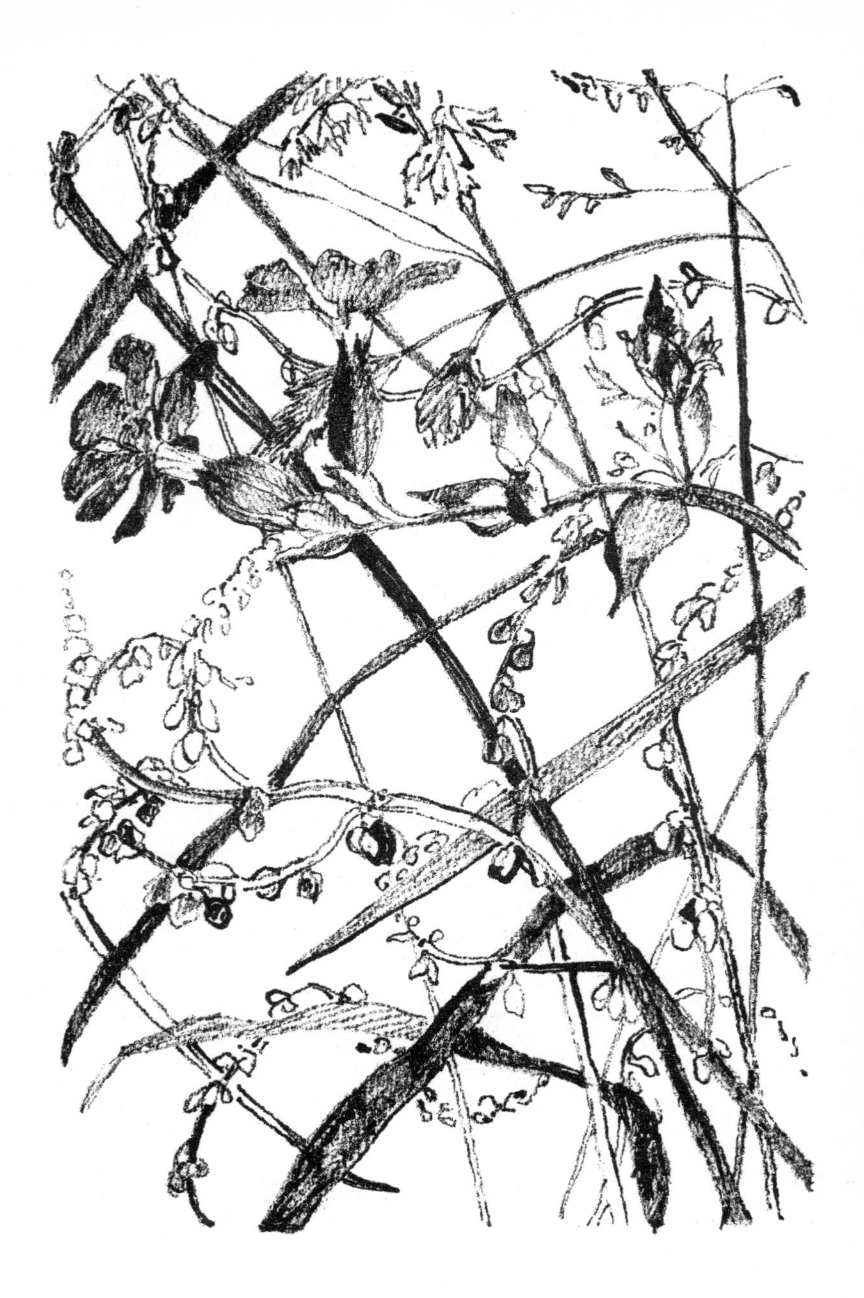

IN FROM THE FIELDS: JOHN CLARE IN WESTMINSTER ABBEY, JUNE 1989

Weave an arch for a nave of grass;
The choristers free birds;
And butterflies be a tapestry:
All testaments to the words

Of one thinking he Byron might be,
Yet sang of hedgerow things –
Of clock-a-clays, thrush break-of-days
And landrails with earth-brown wings.

He knew brief fame for his humble name;
But here is his lasting stone;
And the fields have come where the greatest sung
In praise of a singer their own.

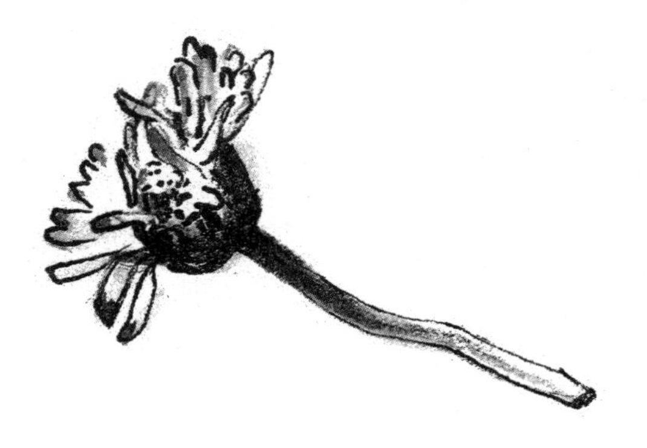

HOLIDAYS

An old French house with green shutters
And flowers flowing like paint
Over arbours and trellises and walks:
Roses and peonies and lupins
Tangled prodigally with
Ducks and hens, a cat and a bustle of pigeons . . .
Here's the water garden with its crooked bridge
And lily leaves like palettes,
And time lies still.

A grey spread of healing stone,
And jackdaws, like black smoke,
The steps – thirty-nine of them –
With their patina of pilgrims,
A red-cassocked choir singing,
And away, away the sea
Glimpsed through the praying fingers
Of wild flowers,
And time lies still.

A big house and a blessing of sunlight,
Flowers trembling with warmth;
And birds everywhere,
Singing unstoppably,
Building and flitting
Through mid-summer's majestic leaves,
Quick in only today,
And time lies still.

COMPENSATION

Without her feline presence
The birds have burgeoned
In a profusion of small, consoling, many-coloured shapes,
Wreathing the garden with song
This long and lavish June.

The flycatcher twists and grabs
On the scented air,
And the wren erupts in a doll's cup of scolding notes,
And the wagtail rears her bobbing tangle of brood,
And owls kee-wick where the white flame of
        moonlight floats.

The nest boxes vibrate with life
And a redstart twirls in his russet;
A pigeon croons and the garden warbler sings,
Its throat pulsating like the throb of the mower . . .
A blackbird joins in with its opera spread of wings.

So soon the full summer's hush,
And heat congealed in the over-laden trees –
The nudge of the sun, high and ever higher,
And baths of foxgloves
Will fill the stifled glade
Where she lies at rest,
And the birds flit at their ease . . .

SILENCE

Silence is company on the long hills –
Buzzard and lark the perfect synthesis;
Tuned into no-noise is eternity's pulse,
A healing that flows and seeps and spills

Through minds muzak-corroded,
Where even Mozart denied is inner peace;
Where the mystic dreams in equal solitude,
And with only bubbling stream moor's quiet eroded . . .

Here the monks in the now sheep-haunted abbey
Troubled the tumbling kite with noise of prayer;
And the clouds were always singing in jubilate
To processions in habits shabby

Where incense waved,
And the quiet at the heart of all
From stone was raised.

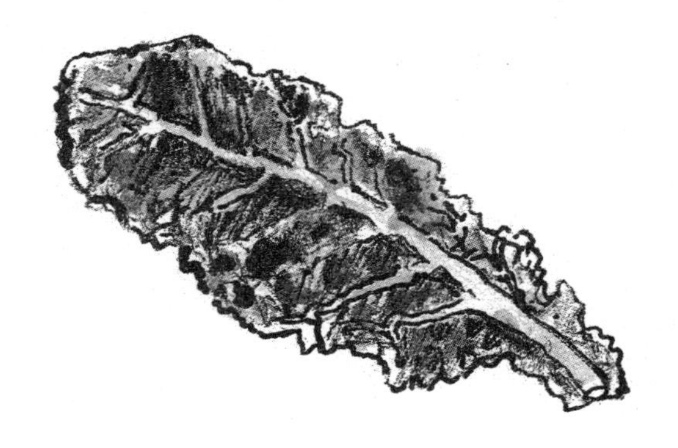

UNSURPRISED VISITOR

Writing a poem mid-afternoon it startled me,
This wet, warm day, October in July,
Rung jerkily from the front, a jangled bell;
Reaching the door, a small blue car slipped by.

Who came, what unguessed opportunity passed?
Romance, or joy, or gain – what thing to sell?
Between the ringing and my answering steps
On the stone outside only two footprints fell:

A listener, with no horse to crop the forest,
A traveller, lost, relieved to see the bell . . .
What chance of reunion, or friends in the making;
Something, on this feigning Autumn day
Only the rooks could tell . . .

ST DAVID'S CATHEDRAL

Lace fingered grass tracery,
Fan vaulting of cowparsley,

Rose windows of campions and scabious,
And banners of sorrel and vetch –
So vulnerable this edifice,
Under its dome of sunlight,
Asking a prayer
From summer-time pilgrims
Who surge in on a tide
Of transistor music and ice-cream wrappers,
To drift away when the sun descends
Horizonwards behind a hot veiling of cloud,
Melting in pink drops
Beyond the thirty-nine steps.

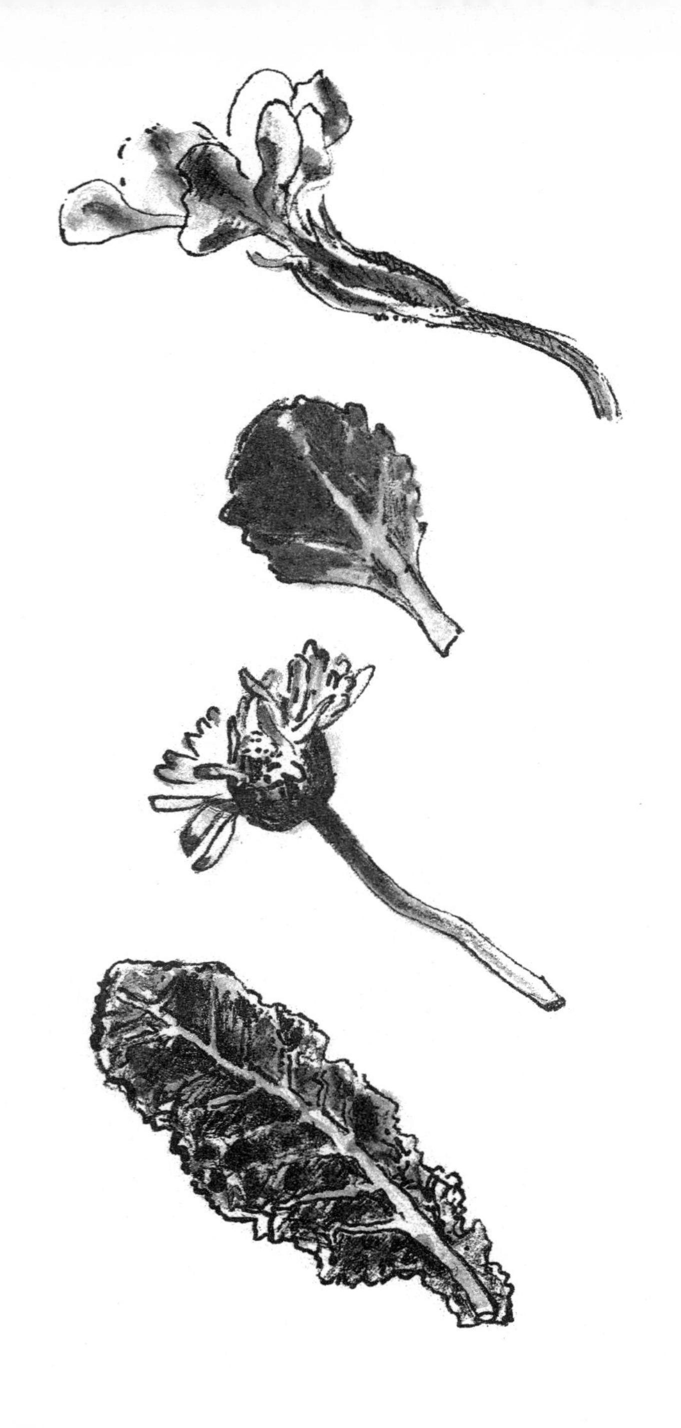

THE LOST ENCHANTMENT

Stay wary in the shadows, my dreams –
I half fear that quick enchantment that seized me
A decade ago, a youth ago
When all seeing was wonder,
And all being a point of enthusiasm;
I want again to rekindle
The magic that was pain and loving,
And yet I fear it so.

Stay wary in the shadows, my dreams,
Insubstantial as spiders' webs,
Yet rock-strong;
Awake again the marvelling
And the white light:
Eternity's ring that only new eyes can see . . .

Yes, I'll accept it, the pain,
To be born again
Where the dark glass lightens imperceptibly
And the nimbus swings . . .

Stay wary in the shadows, my dreams . . .

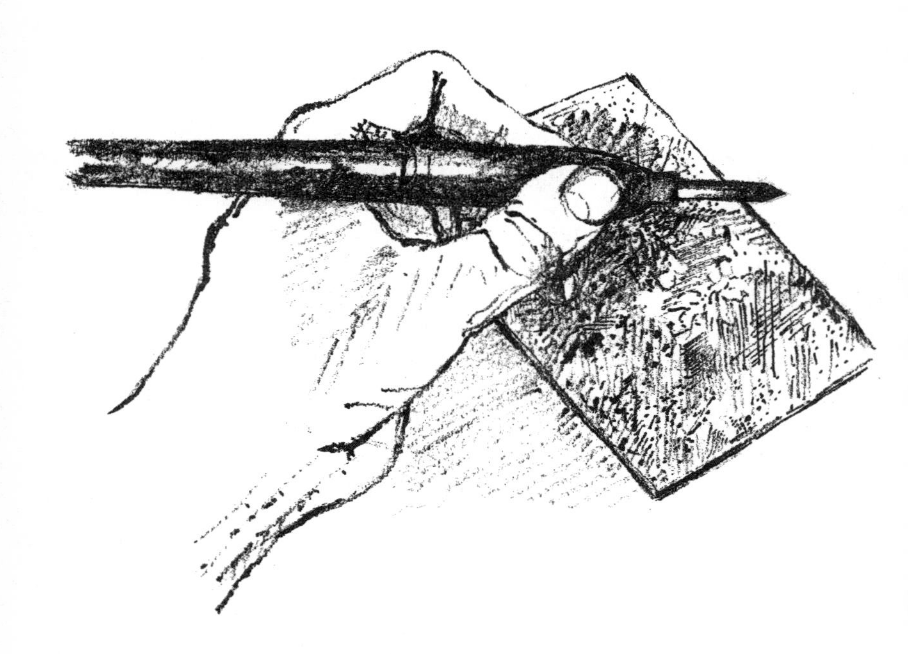

ROBIN TANNER ETCHINGS

Tenderly, nostalgia-tinged,
Undergrowth fringed,
Magic informs his pen,
Conjuring again
A hay-rick, fritillary,
A gate, a tree
Set for a century's span
Among stars beyond probing of man.

Here are birds, wild flowers –
Long hours
Of captured delight
Granted those of chosen sight:
A gift to few . . .
Treasure his world,
For how much longer unfurled?

So little time to impart
His secrets to heal the heart.

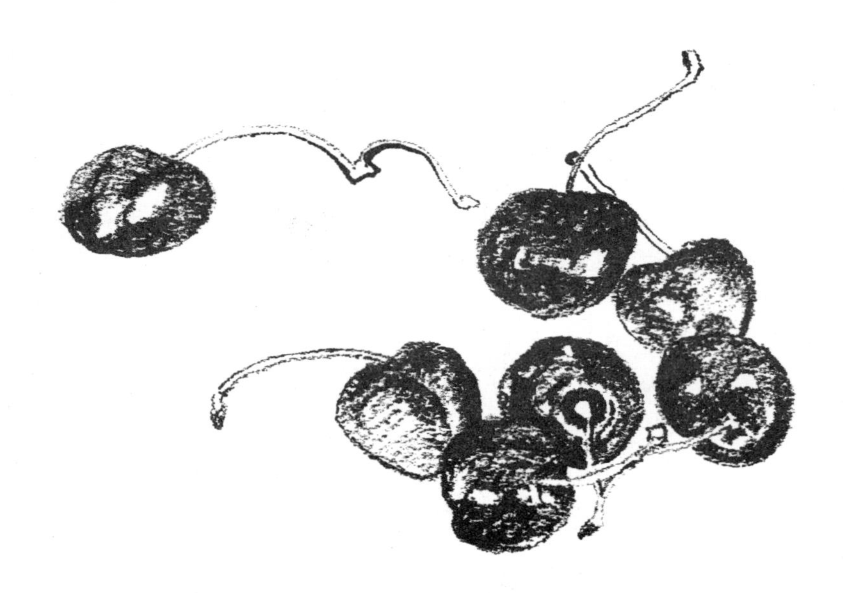

BIRTHDAY

No need for: 'If you'd seen it yesterday'
For fine it was and finer for your coming:
Sun gentle upon the hills, trees
    blossom-fingered,
And everywhere that early summer humming

And tumbling into life . . . A birthday treat
We shared with you in new-eyed countryside.
The day was blessed because it was *your* day –
Memory's gift no parcel could provide.

THE AUDIENCE

Trunks writhing Rackham-like
They leant, listening
To the music older than time –
The jay scolding was only a lost note
In that primeval symphony,
And the wind swathed through the audience,
Unpenetrating
Though it scuffled the ruffled,
Turning leaves
Of the oaks, Rackham-like,
Immutably listening.

TIDES

The tide turns and folk surge in:
Nine-to-five folk,
Fretting in the tight, brown fists
Of banks and shops and offices,
While, outside, the day drips
Golden honey from heaven.

The tide turns and tourists surge in
With overflowing ice-cream cornets,
Looking as floppy, poppy-coloured
As their hats,
Carrying surf boards like giant feet
And buckets bubbling with shrimps . . .

The tide turns and kids surge in,
Garrulous in their schooltime release
As the gulls along the beach,
Pushing, jostling, shooting out
Elbows and tongues, anticipating
        a lack of clothes;
Yearning for mouths full of lollies . . .

The tide turns and dogs surge in.
As the sun burns down to peach
They clip along the sands
In mad tizzies after shied stones,
With flurries out to sea
As hectic as the seals'.

Tide's out. In a fluster of jackdaws
Above the cathedral tower
The village city sleeps.

HORIZONS

The sun swoops upon the sea
And dazzles it up with clouds
In a long line of primrose smoke,
Smudging waveringly into pink and opaque blue
As time encroaches;
And all along the horizon
Silver counters of light dodge and glitter,
Like fish in a net of night,
Combining to the vertical of eternity . . .

There's such a little limit to our
Stretching forth and retreating;
Our journeys and coalescings,
Our grasp of the tangible and
The interactions of dimensions beyond
Time's horizon.
We are dancing to music we cannot hear
Part of a choreography we seldom glimpse
Along sands uncountable . . .
We are partners in the pattern of
An invisible horizon:
Glimmering counters swimming together
Into a planned ocean of tranquillity.

HOUSE

You could tell that good people had lived there –
People who had greatly cared for their
    environment;
For the pure and simple things of life;
People who had benefited their neighbours,
But never pushingly;
People who had minded about a humble heart.

The hills to which they lifted their eyes
Cupped it;
And its garden gave it colours which
Changed with the light.

It had known pain and sorrow,
And birth and death;
But it had a strength
Of its owners' faith
Which was a bulwark to the weary –
You could tell good people had lived there.

Autumn

There's one Sun more strung on my Bead of days.
Henry Vaughan

I travell'd on seeing the hill where lay
My expectation.
George Herbert

His goodness is manifest in making that beauty so delightful and its varieties so profitable. The air to breathe in, the sea for moisture, the earth for fertility, the heavens for influences, the sun for productions, the stars and trees wherewith it is adorned for innumerable uses.

Thomas Traherne

As by some Puddle I did play
Another World within it lay.
Thomas Traherne

STRATA FLORIDA ABBEY

Wing down humble flocks of clouds
Where rushes song of lark
And wagtails dip and flaunt . . .
Here in the twelfth century
Where now thrust through the daisies:
Incense and chants,
Smoking around stoned cloisters;
Fished food,
Sheep tended in fold.
Compassion among the hills,
Like light on a stone-coloured day,
For pack-weary travellers.
Peace, like water on a scorched day,
And the rich poverty of holiness
Thrown everywhere deep, deep
In the sheep-shouldered hills:
A benediction to the edge of time.

COUNTRYMAN

He knew where the pheasants fed
And the half-wild cats sheltered
And adopted them all.

Quick, sensitive hands, sand-paper rough
In cold mittens
Soothed any living creature
Injured or neglected.
He knew where the first lamb was dropped
And where the martins built.
He found the first frail snowdrop huddled,
White on green, like spun glass.

He could mend most things,
Fetch and carry for most people;
And lay out any soul-stripped body.
Neighbours trusted their houses to him,
Entrusting him with cats and donkeys and
 church keys
As though they were so many inanimate parcels.

Tan-touched, far-thinking, his was a face
For keeping secrets,
Shared only with his maker.
He walked warily, an Indian among
Contentious chieftains,
And his being was at the heart of the village,
His spare, black-jacketed figure as much a
 part of the place
As a rooted tree with healing leaves . . .

GREAT GRANDMOTHER'S DIARIES

Word embroidery, spiky-fine
To tell of a stable world,
And picnics by the lake;
Of a nursery of growing lives
No outside events could shake;
Each ordered line

Tells of a pact with time,
Where illness and care still came,
But faith and love lapped the brood
And sunshine and rain
Chased on the changing hill
As they reached their prime

Secure as fledgling wren birds
In a nest so densely knit
That the nuclear heart aches
Dreaming of it,
As I type through
A lifeful of words . . .

ALLEGRO FOR TEN THUMBS

Allegro for ten thumbs
Seeking the magic
Through elusive score;
And she listening polite,
Sensitive to torture
Urging me to try
One more, one more.

Bach and Mozart,
Without the emphasis;
Beethoven, rashly attempted, spelt defeat;
And then, unexpected,
A feeling, a mood, of Schumann
Started the Steinway singing,
And a confidence sweet

Spread, swimming unaided
Out of my depth
In a pool of notes and bars,
Crotchets and quavers,
Speaking an equal progress,
Like a compass charting a dazzle of stars.

She caught delight,
And relief flowed from her,
Giving a plangent force
To the new-found notes;
And the fingers yearned again
For dextrous magic
Beyond the scope
Of mundane typewriter's croak.

ISLAND

So Neptune bugled a hornpipe to it,
My long lost, far alone island
Floating on top of the warm clear water
Where prickly things lie asleep,
Washed to clean bones;
And drunken sailors
Lure down forgotten fins of mermaids
And corals claw to death
Young, godlike poets . . .

And a long, lean ladder of seaweed hair
Tosses across an ever-shifting seabed
In God's thousand ages evening;
And the ocean sounds
Like Welshmen's thousand voices
Above the Caliban-wild storms.

Swing away; out away from toxic wastes
And glutinous oil slicks,
You pink-fresh young sailors,
Here where the shells star
The white sands in stitches of colour
And the waters are green, green, green
When the book is thrown away . . .

NOT THE FACE FOR SONNETS

She hadn't got the face sonnets were written to –
It was a withholding face,
Not without an intimation of the mystic's;
Downrightly sensitive.
Her bones all belonged in the right places,
But scrambled together a little – not classical.
If you'd said her expression was beautiful she'd
Have disbelieved you,
And she had a forgettable face;
Yet while she was with you that
Was what you forgot . . .
A mother, not a mistress;
An everyday, not a Sunday special . . .
Yes, too comfortable a face for sonnets –
Only incoherent lines –
A son might cry for you after dark.

MOLE

Ted Hughes and Our John
Would have had him gutted –
Observed him as a worn-out glove.
He pushed up so crammed with life
Under the dog's exploring nose
From the oozy grass of the bank,
Like a midget slate-coloured dynamo,
Blind as a kitten, oblivious to danger,
His dry, pink claws crampons among
The malleable moss.
We followed the dog to see him;
But, in nature's instant exposure,
He was come and gone –
So sightlessly quick
This fur and vivid bone.

STRAY

He stared in at me through the french window
As gloweringly ill-wishing
As any witch's cat,
His eyes hardly visible
In his raggedy black skull.

When I tapped the window
He started away
With the same alarm
As a blackbird might feel
At his cunning coming.

I was mourning my feline loss,
Who had been my Dives
To his Lazarus . . .
Four-walled,
I felt too safe
And well-fed
As this survivor stared in at me,
Cruelly chilled as he was,
Outside the french window,
Out in the rain,
Each lean, evil bone aching.

COTSWOLD FOUR O'CLOCK

A green-brown, September four o'clock
In a scatter-down of leaves,
A bare bump of tractors . . .
Broken necklaces of berries,
The pond plop of watery things
And self-indulgent gloating over
Awaiting muffins;
Children fizzing from school;
Grandmothers creaking in their gardens;
Dogs guarding breath-stopping bonfires.

Here's the mobile library,
Grinding like a book-full caterpillar
    up the splashy road,
And the bus groaning home,
With its complement of mop-haired pensioners,
From the market town;
Here's the postman
In his Dinky toy van,
Neat as a folded handkerchief . . .

Here are the ducks,
Flopping, feather-shedding
From the dogs and children,
And the cats ingratiating themselves,
Moon-eyed for food . . .

School's out, moorhens are out, doves are out
This fluttering, sun-mazed,
Dahlia-haunted,
Butterflied,
September four o'clock.

FIRE

It was the first thing
To send fear dancing
Down the spines of the animal kingdom –
Dread stronger even than the smell of man;
And man watched the wavering flame,
Bright as another companion,
And warm with crackling chatter.

But when the wind licked up sparks
And lighted the forest
Man knew the animals' fear
Of a force of brutal intransigence
And worshipped it, insignificantly helpless.

Winter

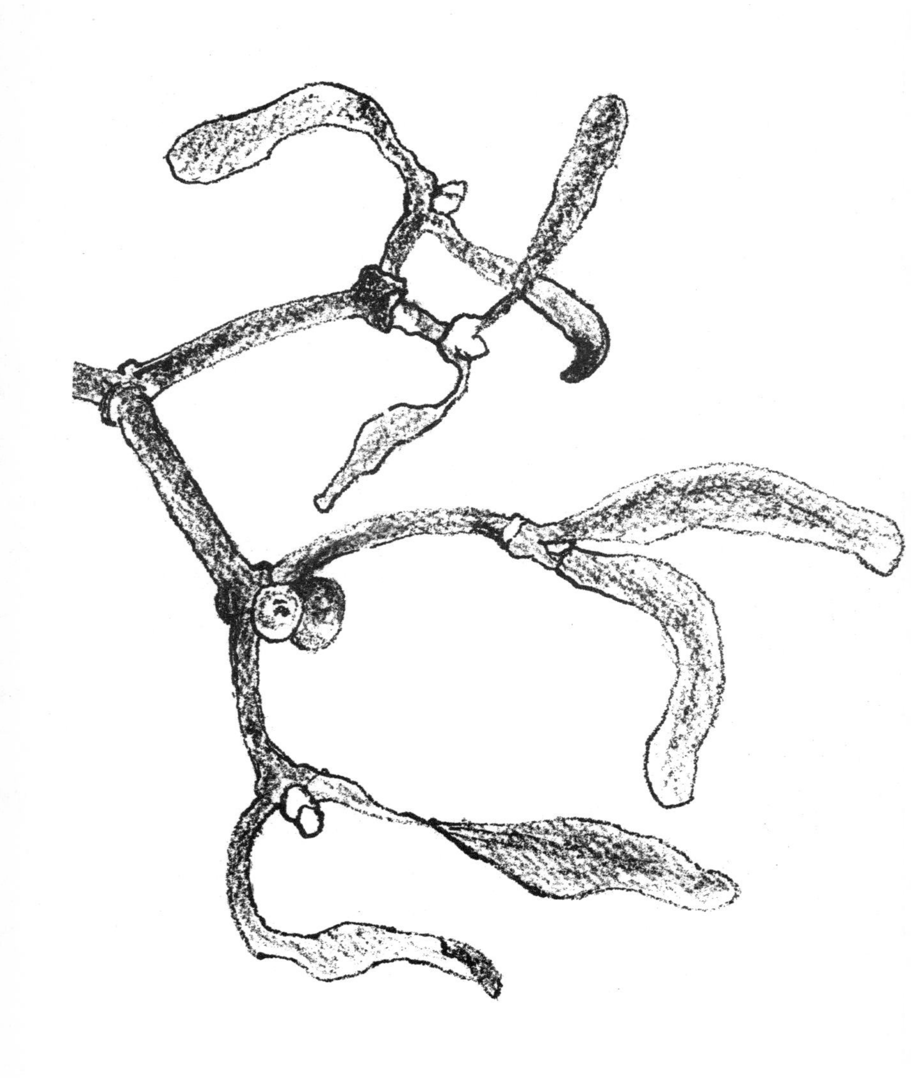

Tempests are calm to thee; they know thy hand,
And hold it fast, as children do their fathers,
Which cry and follow. Thou hast made poore sand
Check the proud sea, ev'n when it swells and gathers.
George Herbert

And here in dust and dirt, O here
The lilies of his love appear!
Henry Vaughan

Whether I flie with angels, fall with dust,
Thy hands made both, and I am there:
Thy power and love, my love and trust
Make one place ev'rywhere.
George Herbert

O here His goodness evermore admire!
He made our souls to make His creatures higher.
Thomas Traherne

THE FORTUNATE

Dustily pecking
Saunter my stray-laying hens,
Sheepdog drilled and free.

SUNDAY

Were you brought up to Sunday?
The given extolling the Giver.
Dusty books and special clothes,
And the blue light and the blood light
Dripping inexorably together through the high windows,
Where candles strive with the sun
In centuries competition.

Do you give in to Sunday?
Track suits and coffee,
And pyramids of contentious papers
Ready to engulf you in a grubby embrace of newsprint . . .
The telly and roast beef
And friends arguing into the new week.

Or do you endure Sunday?
The last cigarette smoked,
The last bag of sugar empty in the cupboard.
Unelated by the Box
And stranded in the city,
Where the rain washes peopleless streets
Occasionally hosing down a mud-coloured mackintosh.

Maddening and gladdening,
Soulful or saddening,
Sunday is special – an oasis dividing
Sloppy Saturday from Mammon's Monday.

ROBIN

Fine-boned and shy, like the gentle impala
Her brush so loved to immortalise,
She treasured all things of beauty;
And her spirit was with the rare,
And the small perfections that many overlooked;
She knew the murmurings of woods in leaf;
The plants and mosses
Most people walked over;
The poems and legends that spoke to the heart.
Her way was so much with the light
That the light claimed her
As a thing of itself.

NO QUICKENING OF PULSES

The 'greenhouse' birds sing in a
Tumbled jumble of tone,
And primroses and daisies spangle
The gardens with beadings of spring;
And the rain has a deceptive livingness,
Making mackintoshes dead weight.

Can it be the beginning of something
New and vital?
My heart waits for a recharged beat of rhythm,
And, for a moment, something warm and precious
Stirs again,
But when I try to recapture
That telescoped past decade
When couplets were sonnets
I stare time in the face,
And acknowledge that
This is ineluctable midwinter.

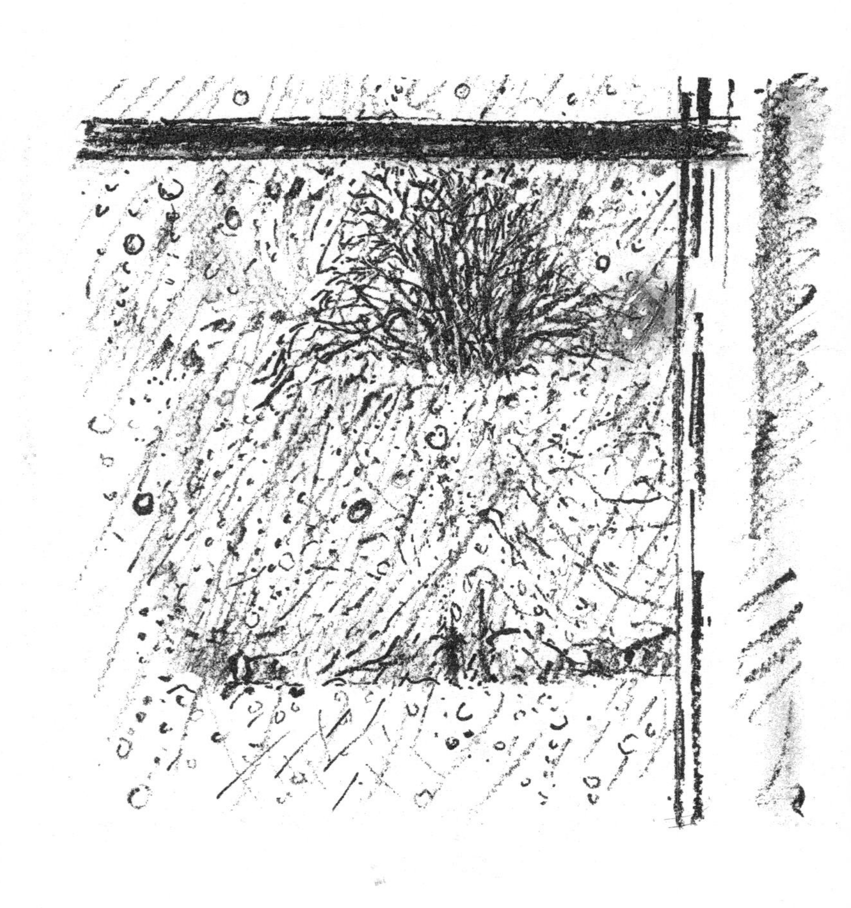

WINTER RAIN

Hear the rattle and gush of it
Lashing the gutters, hammering the skylight
Like a man with twenty fingers;
Shouting through the storm-drenched night
With a manic voice;
Forcing the leaves off the trees
And tossing them down in sodden paper strips,
Beating everything to a chronic wetness . . .

In the country lanes mud trenches thick;
In the town water-swilled pavements
And leaf-strangled gutters
Under the hallowe'en glare of the street lights.

LEAVES

Eau-de-nil, light-soft like lovers' fingers;
Deep, richly flaccid in summer's hush;
Crisply brown, like cracked leather,
And black and pulpy, squashed sodden with rain,
Like unlifted faces,
Until in tall green velvet,
Amidst a drift-down of pin-sharp needles,
The forest tree
Rises up, up, soap-bubble iridescent,
A little afraid of its magic . . .

AFTER THE MEETING

The release blows round in frost breaths
On the star-chained night.
Under the sour glare of the street light
Numbed limbs recover from the child-sized
    chairs;
Tactful minds untangle themselves
After negotiating Easter offerings
And the new churchwardens
Whose throats are still parched from the
    powerful tea.

Cars munch gravel, and the dark hills
Fold round the school's cube of light and
    the inky church
Like parental arms.
Mother Church?
That's it, then . . .
Laughter and an earful of car radio
And the Box at home, waiting.

OWL

I sit on the stone step
And look at my feet –
I am not a baker's daughter –
My swivel head is swarming with thoughts:
I am thinking of deaths
And the ends I will bring
To the mice and the rabbits and the
    young birds.
All day my thoughts have exalted me
While the singing things taunted me:
The blackbird, the thrush and the tit.
There I, impervious sat
While the glare of it:

The light on the song
Dazzled my cat-gold eyes . . .
Now, in the dusk in my silk,
I meditate on surprise.

BOY AND BONFIRE

Garlanded with smoke
He stood in the blank, white day
Like a Joan Hassall woodcut,
Or a Reynolds Stone engraving,
Poking at a nub of flame
Which leapt to colour
From the parchment pattern
Of the captive dancer leaves:
Spent colour in a no-colour day.

So summer dreams drift away
Into monochrome winter reality –
Across the garden
Only the un-frost-touched roses
Lift their heads
Heavy with the soft certainty of Christmas.

CHRISTMAS MARKET

People move slowly, looking steadied-down by
    a Saturday lack of impulsion
After the upbeat of the week
And the manic advertising,
And the Advent calendars and the Cake.
They've just started to feel in the ambush
    of Christmas;
And geniality is gradually creeping through to them
Like water from a warm bath.
Smiles proliferate like the dawning of a myriad
    sunrises . . .

Here's mistletoe in a waxy glimmer of green
    and cream,
And glass balls, one squeeze away from breakage;
And the trees for a hundred living rooms,
Bristling with ephemeral needles,
Pungent as a gasp of tangerine, spiced with
Furniture polish . . .

We're on the edge of Christmas –
On the edge of peace. Can we believe that
Along with all the other things we
Are urged to believe in at Christmas?
Does peace come with a fat, red-clad figure
With a beard white as mistletoe?
Or as a baby born as a refugee and cradled
In scented, cattle-blown hay?
Can it ever really come from two
Fallible men talking, talking continents away?
Today goodwill rises in a dove-flurry of mist
Along the humped-over valley,
It drifts through the Saturday morning Market
Over the people with their cold-apple cheeks,
This frost-radiance as old as time.

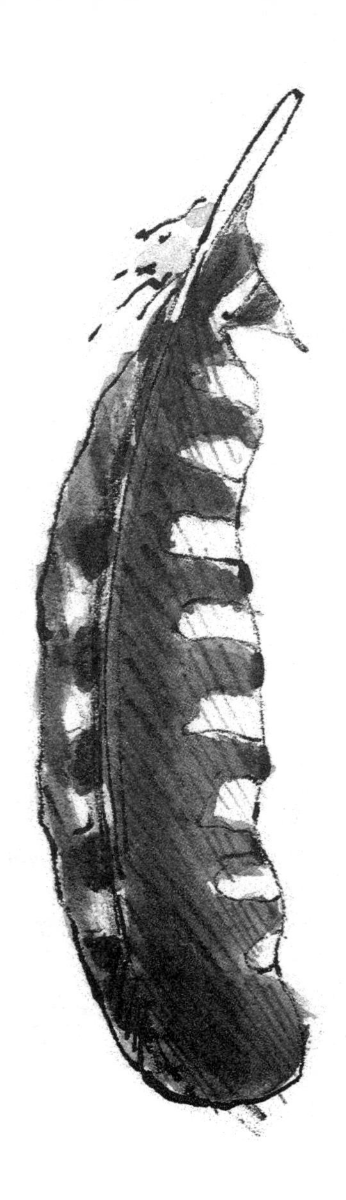

HER SMALL SQUARE OF IVORY

Miss Jane Austen, round-cheeked, robin-bright,
What are you dreaming in the candle light . . . ?
Of dancing with Ben Lefroy all the star-struck
night?

In your frilled cap as your spinster days flit by
Were you a 'husband hunting butterfly'?
Or was Miss Mary Mitford merely being sly?

Quick, the door is creaking – hide away your quill;
Look instead at Fanny's tale on the window sill,
For Aunt Jane remains literary pundit still . . .

Mouse-small stitched embroidery lying on
your knee –
You're now ready to receive any company,
Tucked aside the tell-tale page you scribbled on
with glee.

Your astringent talent gained its force from
stealth –
Foibles and jealousies recorded with youth's
health;
Sister, aunt and daughter, you were loved without
world's wealth . . .

Miss Jane Austen, with your bird-bead eye,
Did your partners mockery sense
As waltzing you swung by?

WORD MANIFEST

A visionary night: stars like flowers,
And the one star loveliest
To point to the Star of Heaven;
The streams hushed in worship
And the angel-struck shepherds
Committing their flocks to the protection
Of the newborn Shepherd . . .

The word rings round of goodwill among men
To a weary world crazed
With man's posturings;
And the kings come
Swept on by Gabriel's wings . . .

Child and Godhead both
Revealed in blazing truth.

Epilogue

DAYTIME

All day and children playing
In the white lengthening light
Of spring;
And the full unexplored wealth of
　　experience
Unwinding like rolls of film
On a camera.

Half day – shadows beginning to grope,
Crouchbacked, across the summer sun;
Prescient perception –
A reconciliation of what was with
What might have been.

End day – the ashy sundown of the
Autumn evening;
All burnt away the care and desire,
Only the shell of life
Fought for to the last bonfire spark.

Winter – the first and last things;
Eyes hope-bright as candles
At the immanence of a child;
Fields watching for the shepherds' song
Over the dark re-creating earth . . .

The Welsh Border Poets

GEORGE HERBERT (1593–1633) was born in Montgomeryshire. His mother was a friend and patron of John Donne. He was a King's Scholar at Trinity College, Cambridge, and in 1616 became a Major Fellow. He was elected a Reader in Rhetoric in 1618, and was obliged by the terms of his fellowship to take orders within seven years. In 1624 and 1625 he represented Montgomery in Parliament and was ordained deacon in 1624. He was installed Canon of Lincoln Cathedral in 1626, and Prebendary of Leighton Bromswold, Huntingdon. He became Rector of Bemerton in 1630. When he was dying he sent his poems to his friend Ferrar to be published. *The Temple*, containing nearly all his poems, appeared in 1633: 'A picture of the many spiritual conflicts that have passed betwixt God and my soul before I could subject mine to the will of Jesus my Master.'

THOMAS TRAHERNE (1637–1674) was born in Hereford, the son of a shoemaker. He went to Brasenose College, Oxford in 1653. He was Rector of Credenhill, Herefordshire, and was ordained in 1660. He wrote *The Centuries* for Susanna Hopton. He gained a BD in 1669, and became Chaplain to Sir Orlando Bridgeman. He expresses an innocent joy in creation, influenced by Neoplatonism.

HENRY VAUGHAN (1621–1695) was born at Newton upon Usk, Breconshire. He was one of twins. In 1638 he went to Jesus College, Oxford, and in 1638 he went to London to study law. He returned to Breconshire at the outbreak of the Civil War when he was clerk to Marmaduke Lloyd and possibly fought as a Royalist. He may have had a profound religious experience when his brother died. He may have practised medicine from the 1640s. He was seized with the idea of childish innocence, as Traherne was, and called himself a Silurist, because his native Brecon was anciently inhabited by the British tribe of Silures.

Adapted from Margaret Drabble's *Oxford Companion to English Literature*, 1985.

Also published in Spire:

A Journey into God *Delia Smith*

A profound reflection on a subject of deep personal significance to Delia Smith: prayer.

'A useful and practical guide.' *The Sunday Times*

'A book for the non-believer and, perhaps even more so, for the not-quite-believer – and this must include an awful lot of us.' Barry Norman

'It is like having a wise, practical friend on the same wavelength.' Lional Blue

Searching for God *Cardinal Basil Hume*

Cardinal Hume discusses the problem facing anyone who attempts to obey the twofold command to love both God and neighbour.

'Heartwarming and inspiring – a classic.' *Coventry Evening Telegraph*

'Practical and down-to-earth, concerned not with abstract theories but with daily difficulties.' *The Times*

The Restless Heart *Ronald Rolheiser*

'Loneliness is not a rare and curious phenomenon. It is at the centre of every person's ordinary experience.' This outstanding book will reassure and free many to life more meaningfully.

'This is not a book to read for an answer to all the problems of loneliness, but for the ability of the author to move us from the danger of the condition to its immense opportunities.' Dr Jack Dominian

'I read this book with a mounting sense of recognition.' Richard Holloway, Bishop of Edinburgh

Forgotten among the Lilies *Ronald Rolheiser*

Ronald Rolheiser comments on our struggle to move 'beyond our obsessions, restlessness, fears and guilts, that rob us of the spirit of our own lives, of the feel of our own cold and warmth, of the taste of our own coffee, and the consolation of God.'

'Ronald Rolheiser invites us to look beyond the surface of our lives. He gives us permission to be human. He is a gifted communicator and I personally value his writings very much.'
Delia Smith